40 DAYS OF WORSHIP: THERE MUST BE A DEATH

TANEKA YOUNG

DEDICATION

This book is dedicated to my Lord and Savior Jesus Christ for without him this would not have been made possible. I also dedicate this to my four beautiful children, Ahzontaye, Jarius, Kobey and Saniyah for believing in me and hanging in there when times were not so pleasant. Thank you for your sacrifice, unconditional love and for dying to yourself. Without you motivating me to finish, we would not be here today. I love you with all of my heart and this is just the beginning. You guys are the real MVPS.

Table of Contents

Introduction

When it comes to worship, no one automatically thinks of death. Most people think of music and five people standing before a congregation singing songs to usher in the presence of the Lord. That can be easily interpreted as such but we must go deeper than the surface. Death is a part of worship and must be done daily in order to please God how he sees fit. When Jesus came down from heaven, his purpose was to redeem us back to our rightful place. By him coming and lowering himself, he laid down who he was and became who we needed. It wasn't always easy but he understood the importance of death. It is necessary if we want to accomplish the will of God in the earth. No flesh can enter into the kingdom of God so we must mortify our earthly members and present our bodies as a living sacrifice.

Losing someone is never easy and sometimes we focus more on the death than the resurrection. Lazarus died and all they could think about was him no longer being with them. If they truly knew who Jesus was, when he showed up they would have known that life was about to return.

Dying to yourself is allowing life to come forth not only in you but the life of those that are around you. Without it, so many people would be lost and we would not be able to experience the fullness of God for whom he truly is. You must come ready to give up yourself because it's appointed unto man to die but to die is to gain eternal life.

During the next 40 days, you will experience a period in time where you present yourself as the living sacrifice. In order to obtain that which God has promised, you must be willing let go and let God. It is during this process that many do not make it out of because it requires them to look at themselves in the mirror. If God is going to use you, you can no longer be the person in control. He deals with your character and in that you find out what is important and what isn't. God desires to use those who choose not to think more highly of themselves than they ought and are willing to put others in front. It may not always be easy to be the bigger person, but reward is greater for those who choose the lesser seat in the kingdom. Jesus was brought low in order to raise us up. Are you willing to do the same? Let's take a look at what he is requiring from us all.

Day 1

What is the Lifestyle of Worship?

"But the hour cometh, and now is, which the true worshippers shall worship the Father in spirit and in truth; for the Father seeketh such to worship him." John 4:23 KJV

We live in a society which tells us that praise and worship is a position in the church. We associate worship with singing and the moving of the feet therefore raising a generation on emotionalism and not truth. When you look up the word worship in the dictionary, it means reverence or devotion to a deity, intense love or admiration of any kind. It also means to set apart for a special use or service, to give up (of one's self or one's time, energy, etc.) to some purpose, activity or person.

Worship is the denying of your flesh and operating in the spirit. A worship leader is not the lead singer on the praise and worship team but it is a lifestyle. Worship is being the sacrifice and offering up you to be used by God in any way at any time. Worship is being separate from the world and keeping the commandment that God has asked of us. A worshiper walks and operates in love. Worshipers do not waver but stand strong on the word of God and the things concerning God. Worshipers give up their will for the will of the Father. They do not seek the things of this world but always minding the things that are above.

They are not ashamed of the Gospel by honoring him with reverence and they have no other God before him. They agree with God and take his word and operate through faith. There is always a yes in a worshiper. He is looking for people who will deny themselves, take up their cross and follow him. Worship is what God honors. He is looking for total commitment. When we submit to a lifestyle of worship, it is at this time that we are able to walk away from people, places and things that will cause us to not give God all of us. Once we make up in our minds to give it all we have, we will begin to live according to the example Christ has set before us.

Today's application: One must be willing to take a good look at their relationship with Christ. You must ask the hard questions and be ready to look you in the face. Dying is never easy but if you are serious about your future with God, this is necessary. Make it personal and start with you today. Admittance is the first step to recovery.

Day 2

Worship is for the Mature

"When I was a child, I spoke and thought and reasoned as a child. But when I grew up, I put away childish things. I Corinthians 13:11 NLT

Mature means to continue developing to desired level. One thing you must realize is that maturity doesn't always come with age. It is a mindset we develop by applying the lessons that we learn. Maturity is continuous growth in a desired direction. Once we come into the knowledge of Christ, our worship should always be maturing.

Immature worship limits us and keeps us with a childlike attitude. It throws tantrums when it doesn't get what it wants and it reacts in a way that keeps the focal point on self and away from others. Mature worship keeps its eye on the prize and facing forward. Immature worship is emotional and liable to change at any given moment. God needs consistent mature worshipers who understand the importance of reaching others. We must press to always have a heart of mature worship so that our lights will draw men and women to Christ.

It can no longer be all about us. God requires so much more from us because we have been given so much. Once we answer the call, we have entered into a different realm that can no longer cater to just us. We must take our eyes off of ourselves and see the big picture. Christ died for us all. If all we can think about is how someone wronged us, we have forgotten how much we wronged Christ. It's time to grow up.

Today's application: When you are overlooked for a position, are you easily offended? Throughout the day, look for opportunities to speak highly of someone else. Recommend them for a position. Show others that you can handle their success because you understand what it means to be there for one another.

Day 3

Unconditional Worship

"But God commanded his love toward us, in that while we were yet sinners, Christ died for us." Romans 5:8 KJV

Worship is a voluntary lifestyle dedicated unto the Lord. It should be done freely and without restrictions. It is not dependent upon any particular thing and is given from the heart. When God looks at us, it is through the eyes of righteousness. He freely gives us all things and he showed us when he gave us his only begotten son. He did not withhold him until we got it all together. While we were yet sinners, Christ died for us and before we were in our mother's womb, he became the way for us.

We must be mindful that we are not worshiping from a state of prerequisites. We should not make demands upon God in order for us to cooperate. The releasing of our worship is not modified or restricted by reservations. Worship is built upon trust and faith. We follow through with what God has asked of us because we are confident in his character. We can give of ourselves completely because we know that his word is true. When we try to negotiate with God to get him to prove himself before we offer up ourselves through worship, we have started functioning through manipulation and a characteristic tied to self-worship. God's love towards us is never through conditions and once we put limits on our worship, we cheapen the experience with him and deny him access to all of us.

Today's application: Don't wait until someone does something for you before you do something for them. Worship freely gives of itself. Don't hold back because others may not give their all. You do what's right and pleasing in the eyes of God. He sees and he will repay.

Day 4

Love Thy Neighbor

"And the second is like unto it, Thou shalt love thy neighbor as thyself." Matthew 22:39 KJV

One of the commandments God has given us is to love our neighbors as ourselves. He commands us to love one another for he is love. We should always be concerned about our brothers and sisters no matter what the circumstance may be. Worship will keep our eyes on the needs of others.

We cannot effectively worship God and neglect those in need. We should be just as concerned about them as we are about ourselves. Those who are strong in the faith should be ready to lift those who are weak. We should always be available to give a word in love so that they will keep running this race and endure until the end. We should never take pleasure in the downfall of others. Our love for God will always put us in the position to lend a helping hand. God honors those who are less concerned about their needs and more concerned about the needs of others.

Loving them may not always be easy but with Christ all things are possible. God is looking at his children to see how they will respond. Now that we have been adopted into his family, he has a certain standard that his children must uphold. He is not concerned about what goes on in the house of the neighbor but what we show them while we are in their presence. We can't control the actions of others and he doesn't ask you to. He commands us to show his love no matter what they say or do. We must remember the Lord will fight for us. Be still and know that he is God.

Today's application: It is hard to love someone you don't like. Their ways may not be your first choice but by being the light, you can help guide them in the right direction. Don't be so quick to give up on your neighbor, co-worker or your family. Someone loved you back to life. Don't forget to extend that same grace and mercy.

Day 5

Forgiving and Forgetting Brings Movement

"No, dear brothers and sisters, I have not achieved it, but I focus on this one thing: Forgetting the past and looking forward to what lies ahead." Philippians 3:13 NLT

In order to go forward, we must be willing to forgive and forget. Now I know we are wondering how we are supposed to do that. Many of us have been wronged in ways that most people would not believe us if we told them. The pain of our past can be a bit much and forgiving is the last thing we intended upon doing. It takes a new level of maturity to forget the pain inflicted from someone else. Many people say they can forgive but they won't forget.

Forgiving others gives us the ability and opportunity to live again. We must be willing to let ourselves out of the cage we continue to hold ourselves in. Unforgiveness is a self-inflicted gunshot wound that we give ourselves which causes us to lose the blood that is vital to our existence. Without the blood, we are dying slowly and remaining in a place that we desire to get up from but are too weak to do it. We miss out on so much and God can't get the glory out of our lives if he can't get us to move. Getting through the hurt and pain is never easy but we must ask ourselves how bad we want it.

We must be intentional about forward movement. Stagnation comes from an emotional place and the need to hold on to moments in our lives that are not beneficial to our greater. It is during this time guilt will come to get us to stay put. Guilt is a tool the enemy uses to keep us from fulfilling our assignment for God. We must recognize it and push through because if we entertain it too long, we will become a part of the act.

If something or someone is behind us, it means we kept going and they took a break. Don't slow down because they were not equipped properly for the journey. We are not responsible for their momentum. At some point they will either catch up or drop out completely. Either way, keep going and do not stop.

Our opportunities are available but if we allow what's behind you to dictate to you what's ahead, we will miss out on the greatest move of God in our lives. God is not concerned with who will be left behind. He's concerned with who will miss out if we don't go. We only hold a grudge when we think they have won. Forgiveness can come when we become confident that we have the victory because God is on our side. Jesus was able to forgive because he understood who he was and what God had already spoken over his life. The enemy is already defeated because we belong to God and he will bring to pass all that he ordained. We can forgive once we know who we are and whose we are. Forgiveness is a part of our lifestyle, not a onetime event.

Today's application: Forgive quickly and move on. Do not give the enemy any room to come in and allow the offense to fester. Address it and keep it pushing. The more you think about it, the more you will remain stuck and will not be able to produce any fruit. Allow God to deal with them. Keep your hands clean and watch God work it out in you favor in the near future.

Day 6

Distracted Worship

"Give all your worries and cares to God, for he cares for you. I Peter 5:7" NLT

Our lives are filled with so much. Whether it's our children, spouse, job, church duties or just everyday errands, we are pretty busy. We find ourselves running most days and hardly have time to rest before we are off to complete another to do list. If we add distractions to our day, our mind is totally off balance and nothing gets done. We start to feel as though we have failed because nothing seemed to get accomplished.

In the spirit, distractions come to keep us from focusing on the assignment that has been placed upon our lives. They come at the most inconvenient times but yet they get paid the most attention. The enemy knows what will get us off our rocks and will use it against us every time. If we are distracted, our focus has now been turned towards us and we all know that things are downhill from there. As much as we try to shift our focus, it's too late and we have fallen for it.

There are no such things as a good distraction, no matter what the circumstances are. Even if we use a distraction to get our mind off of something, we have not dealt with the problem and we will remain in a state of self. We can't allow the distractions to control our lives. We must be able to focus and complete our assignments. We have to give our distractions to God. While we are trying to fix it, we are neglecting our duties as a worshiper.

Today's application: Limit the number of things you add to your plate. The less you have on it, the more you can focus on what you need to do. Being busy is not always a good thing because it separates you from what's important. God did not call us to be busy, but fruitful. Make sure your time is being spent building others and not just yourself.

Day 7

Renewed Mind

"Don't copy the behavior and customs of this world, but let God transform you into a new person by changing the way you think. Then you will learn to know God's will for you, which is good and pleasing and perfect." Romans 12:2 NLT

Our thought process affects us in so many ways. We have been told that a mind is a terrible thing to waste and whatever a man thinketh, so is he. It is the mind that shapes our worlds each and every day. Our battles are fought in the mind and that is where God speaks to us and the enemy speaks at us. If we do not have a sound mind, we will be unstable in all of our ways.

We all have faced many things in our lives that have caused us to move, breakout or shrink back. Our minds must be renewed and transformed so that we can give the best of us at all times. However we feel and think about ourselves is how we will respond. Worship is about giving and if we believe we have nothing to give, then opportunities will come and go and the glory of God will not be visible in the life of a believer. The mind is the highest part of our bodies and it controls every move we make. Spiritual wickedness is going on in high places. We must be careful not to allow the enemy free reign in our thoughts. If the mind doesn't believe it, worship won't be achieved and breakthrough can be delayed or denied.

Today's application: Think on things that are true, pure and honest. Those thoughts come from keeping the mind stayed on Jesus. When you have peace, it because you have taken your mind off of what you see and placed it on what you know is of God. Keeping your mind occupied with him will allow you to receive the words he speaks concerning your life.

Day 8

Division is not Worship

"I appeal to you, dear brothers and sisters, by the authority of our Lord Jesus Christ, to live in harmony with each other. Let there be no divisions in the church. Rather, be one mind, united in thought and purpose." I Corinthians 1:10 NLT

A house divided will not stand. Divorce is the separation of what was once one back to two. Disagreements can some time put us on the opposite sides of the tracks. Opinions can lead to separation and division hurts more than it helps.

Unity is where we are with accord with a common goal to achieve. Our goal in worship is to bring God's will into the earth. The moment we decide that we are going to continue to do our own thing, we have allowed division to separate us from his purpose. Jesus said in John 10:30 that he and the Father are one. They do not function separate from each other and if we are going to live the life as Christ followers, our mission is to live as one with each other.

Our worship should never bring division to the body of believers. We should strive to live peacefully with all men. Uniting brings the power of God into our atmosphere which in turn will bring change into the lives of those we are sent to help.

Today's application: Just like worship is for the mature, so is unity. What are you bringing with you when you come into the room? Is it life or death, unity or division? Wherever you may go today, bring the unity with you. It does not matter if no one else wants to hold hands and sing with each other. Make sure you leave a sweet fragrance in the atmosphere. God is watching and he is looking for those who worship in spirit and in truth at all times.

Day 9

Worship is an Asset, not a Liability

"We use God's mighty weapons, not worldly weapons, to knock down the strongholds of human reasoning and to destroy false arguments." 2 Corinthians 10:4 NLT

An asset is a valuable person or thing; something useful in an effort to foil or defeat an enemy. It is also known as an agent. Our worship in the eyes of God is more than just an exercise. It is a weapon that we use in order to defeat the plot of the enemy.

We are worship agents unto God and when we worship, we are able to destroy the yoke of the enemy. Worship frees others from bondage therefore God honors worship from a pure heart. Worship is valuable and useful in our everyday lives. If we really want to see a move of God, we must see the value in us so that we will have the confidence to free others through our worship.

Worship should never burden us but it should lift the burdens of others that are around us. We are to bear each other's burdens and if we are not able to see past our own circumstances, the worship that is being offered is not pure or from a humbling place. We all have issues that we face but no one should face them alone. Together we are able to destroy the enemy. We are stronger in numbers than we are by ourselves. Our worship should add no sorrow to those we come in contact with.

Today's application: God sees you as a change agent and you are valuable to him. Walk with your head held high knowing that he trust you to get the job done. He needs you to be at your best so that someone can come from under the oppression that has had them bound. You are an asset to the kingdom and we need you to survive.

Day 10

Control Your Actions

"But I say, walk and live habitually in the Holy Spirit, responsive and controlled and guided by the Spirit; then you will certainly not gratify the cravings and desires of the flesh of human nature without God." Galatians 5:16 AMP

Emotions are a part of our everyday lives. We laugh, cry, get angry, feel sad and we get excited. It is through our emotions that we express ourselves when we may not always have the words. Emotions have been around since the beginning of time and will be here until the end.

The fruit of the Spirit that we must learn and apply is temperance or self-control. Being able to control our emotions shows our maturity and dedication to following Christ. When we rely on our emotions to make decisions, we don't give God the opportunity to work through us. Emotions can keep us from moving forward in purpose. When we constantly depend on our emotions to get us through, we hardly get anywhere and no one benefits from someone on a continuous emotional roller-coaster.

We must learn to live and walk in the spirit and become independent from our feelings. We can confuse worship with an emotional encounter and miss God and the opportunity to be a blessing to someone else. Emotions keep us focused on us and what our needs and wants are. Worship is selfless compassion for others and if our feelings are always turned on, our worship is turned off.

Today's application: Pay close attention to what is driving you today. If your emotions are in the drivers' seat, they will react instead of responding. A reaction is not always needed and sometimes no response is the response. Allow the Holy Spirit to guide you on what to say and you will be able to keep your mind focused and your light shining.

Day 11

Let Down Your Guard

Trust in the Lord at all times; ye people, pour out your heart before him: God I'd a refuge for us. Selah. Psalm 62:8 KJV

When I think about a guard, my mind reflects upon the soldiers who stand guard at the tomb of the Unknown Soldier or the guards at Buckingham palace. They are in their positions day in and day, no matter what. They are always on guard and ready to defend their territory. They are committed and dedicated to the cause.

Just like these guards, they are trying to keep people out and maintain control from anyone entering their comfort zone. Many of us have guards in place in order to keep people out and to stay in control. We will go through great lengths to stay in charge and will only allow what we think is possible to take place. We can't worship God from a guarded place. He will never have all of us. He will never be able to pour into us because we're overly cautious about his intentions. Worship is about being free and when we're guarded, we are bound by the thing that we are fighting so hard to protecting ourselves from.

We must give ourselves permission to dismiss our guard. Letting go allows us to enter into a place of rest from worry and doubt. We don't have to defend ourselves or fortify ourselves from God. He desires for us to walk in freedom. A guard will only allow our worship to get so far before he steps in and stops us from flowing in the spirit.

Today's application: Give your guard a break. Give God some time and space to speak to you concerning your guarded areas. If you are holding on to the things that hurt you, God can't pour anything into you and he sure can't get anything out. Start with one area and open up to God about it. He will come in and begin to build it back up with the right things. After he is done, you will never have to protect yourself because now you have the shield and buckler doing it for you.

Day 12

Come Ready to Die

"I beseech you there for brethren, by the mercies of God, that ye present your bodies a living sacrifice, holy, acceptable unto God, which is your reasonable service." Romans 12:1 KJV

When Jesus came down in the human form, he understood what he was coming for. He didn't come to do his own thing. He didn't come just to live in the earth. He didn't come to waste time. He didn't come to heal only. He came to die. He came knowing that through his death, the world might be saved.

When we come to God through worship, we're coming to die. We're telling God that we no longer have the mind to follow our own path. We are voluntarily presenting our bodies as a living sacrifice. We are letting it be known that through our coming and our death, God can use us to save someone else life. We are making a public declaration that our life is not our own. Jesus understood that once his mind was made up to come and die, his life would not be the same. If we are going to worship God, there must be a death.

Today's application: You must present yourself unto God. He will never force you but you must count up the cost. We are not our own and we were bought with a price. You must decide what is more important, your life or the life of others. What does it profit a man to gain the whole world and to lose his soul?

Day 13

Who Lives Within

"Ye are of God, little children, and have overcome them: because greater is he that is in you, than he that is in the world." I John 4:4 KJV

Each day we come in contact with so many different people. We draw conclusions of people based upon what they drive, what they wear and where they reside. We really can't tell much about a person until we have lived with them. This is where we get to see them behind closed doors and where most things are hidden from the world.

Worship is derived from what or who resides on the inside of us. We know that in order to worship God, we must do it in the spirit. If the spirit of God is living on the inside of us, we would live in the spirit. We would respond with love, peace, joy, faith and long-suffering. This is a part of worship.

If we're always responding with hate, envy, jealousies, and malice, we are living according to the flesh. This allows others to see who lives within us. We can't worship God with foolishness residing with us day in and day out. God doesn't honor that. We have to be mindful of who we allow to live with us. We have to stop shacking up with the flesh and live a committed, consecrated life with Christ.

Today's application: A tree is known by the fruit it bears. How you treat people on a daily basis shows them who you are, not them. Make sure that they can see fruit a branch that is connected to the vine. It should be full of life and not death. Nobody wants rotten fruit; neither do they want to be around a fruitless and mean spirited Christian.

Day 14

Insecure Worship

"For ye have not received the spirit of bondage again to fear; but ye have received the Spirit of adoption, whereby we cry, Abba, Father." Romans 8:15 KJV

Insecure worship comes from a place of not being confident in one's ability brought on through fear. People who are insecure shy away from productive ministry. Often times they find themselves doubting their ability in God. Not knowing who we are will cause our worship to become null and void.

Being insecure keeps us secluded and isolated from what God truly wants to do through us. If God reveals to us who we are, we should have the faith to believe he knows what he's talking about. We are now a part of his family and we don't have to be afraid of the person he says we are. Insecurities are one of the quickest ways to damage and end a relationship. The enemy will play on that so you will not get to the place of prosperity and power. Accept what God says so our worship will exude confidence in the one whom we speak about.

Today's application: Fear is an indication that there are still areas that you may still be insecure about. Ask the Father to show you those areas so that it can be brought up by the root. Insecurities will limit your interaction with others and they will miss out on the gifts and talents you possess.

Day 15

Complete not Compete

"And there are diversities of operations, but it is the same God which workers all in all." I Corinthians 12:7 KJV

We all have the ability and the opportunity to worship God and to be all that he has called us to be. We have different gifts and talents inside of us which were placed there by him. God assigned us all something unique to do and we can't do each other's job. Worship is about coming together with our different gifts that are spread out among other believers.

When we begin to compete and compare ourselves with others, we can neglect and reject the very qualities God equipped us with. It can be looked at as a lack of appreciation for the things God has entrusted us with. God sees us all as equal and our equality is in Christ. We should not exalt ourselves higher than others. Worship acknowledges the strengths in others and makes room for them to be displayed. Worship is not about focusing totally on us but being a light so that others may be drawn to Christ.

As we go forth in worship, our gifts are to be used for the perfecting of the saints. We should pour so much into each other that we will see them complete in some areas. The bible declares he who has begun a great work in us is able to complete it. We are striving to become a completed work in Christ. It takes all of us working together to make sure that it comes to pass.

Today's application: See yourself as God sees you. You have just as much as the next person and God desires to use you just like them. Speak positively about yourself and be mindful that you are needed in the body of Christ.

Day 16

Heart Transplant

"A new heart also will I give you, and a new spirit will I put within you: and I will take away the stony heart out of your flesh, and I will give you an heart of flesh." Ezekiel 36:26 KJV

When it comes to the matters of the heart, we are told to guard it because the issues of life flow from it. If we are not careful, we will find ourselves doing things that may be good but not of God. Our heart must be replaced with the heart of Christ in order to achieve the magnitude of love that God wants to flow through us.

Taking on the heart of Christ is to love unconditionally and exchange ours for others. By placing our heart in his hands, we are more compassionate for others and we're not concerned with our heart being abused. He watches over it and out of it is an uninterrupted flow of worship that is a sweet sound in his ear.

Our hearts must be turned toward God and in return, we will have love for others. He writes his law upon our hearts and that is where we hide his word so that we might not sin against him. Without going through the surgery, we will not receive his heart and will continue to function out of an old heart is that still damaged. A new heart guarantees us a worship that will please God at all times.

Today's application: Present your heart to God so that he can do what needs to be done. He will protect it at all times and you will be better than you have ever been before. Don't be afraid to love again for love allows us to pour out of our soul unto a loving and caring Father.

Day 17

Respecting Others

"Respect everyone, and love the family of believers. Fear God, and respect the king." I Peter 2:17 NLT

The golden rule states that we are to do unto others as we would have them to do unto us. This may not always be the case since this world is becoming colder and colder by the minute. God is not a respecter of person and we should not be as well. He is constantly looking for people who will walk up right before him and treat others justly regardless of what they receive in return.

Giving respect only when it's shown to us is the way of the world. We are not of this world so we must show the world how it is to be done. That type of behavior shows our maturity level and how much of us that still has not died. When we carry around those feelings, they will hinder us from sending up a pure praise and from following through with our purpose. There is never a right time to disrespect our neighbor or fellow brother or sister in the Lord. God frowns on arrogance and to continue in it suggests that we are more lifted up then Christ is.

Today's application: Respect is given regardless of the situation. See God in everything even when you have been disrespected. Being able to humble yourself is a sign of maturity and your worship is being honored by God.

Day 18

Check Your Motives

"Take heed that ye do not your alms before men, to be seen of them: otherwise ye have no reward of your Gather which is in heaven." Matthew 6:1 KJV

If you want to see the heart of a person, check their motives. People do many things for many different reasons. During a crime scene, it's often asked what was their MO or main objective. We are driven by what is in our hearts. The bible says wherever a man's treasure is, that is where his heart is.

If worship is in our heart, our motives will be pure. We will point others to God and not to ourselves. We will yield ourselves unto God in order to achieve the level of fulfillment he desires. We should never desire the spotlight nor to be lifted up with applause and praise. If we are constantly holding out for a round of applause from man, we will miss our standing ovation from God.

We should never manipulate situations so that they work in our favor. Always make sure your motives line up with the will of God. Even though it may be a good thing to do, it should not come back up once we think the other person is getting ahead. If we are going to do anything, do it as unto the Lord.

Today's application: Make sure you are able to fulfill the duty you signed up for and that you are doing it because you want to help, not to have something to hold over their head. If you are not able to, don't agree to the terms and then complain to others about it. God sees all and he hears all even when you don't utter a word. Your heart tells on you every time.

Day 19

Consider Your Ways

Haggai 1:7 "Thus saith the Lord of hosts; consider your ways. KJV

In the book of Luke, Jesus stops by the house of Martha and Mary. When we have guest over, we want them to feel comfortable especially if it is Jesus. Martha began to prepare a meal for him and the disciples while Mary went and sat at his feet. Martha begin to complain to him that she was the only one concerned about getting the meal together and Mary needed to come and help her. In that moment, Jesus told Martha that Mary had chosen that which was needful. She put the Lord before anything else.

Through worship, our focus should always be about the building up of his kingdom. If we are always asking God about our house and what will come of our desires, we have allowed self to control our decisions. We often wonder why things are not happening in our lives and that is because we have abandoned what is important and needful. God is not pleased with us leaving him for ourselves. Our worship is of no effect once we put ourselves over what he has asked of us. Is our house getting in the way of his business? Are we only crying out on our behalf and forgetting to cry out for others? He has always supplied our needs. We must remember that we must seek ye first the kingdom and all the other things will be added unto us. Therefore, consider your ways.

Today's application: What have you put before the Lord? What gets more of your attention? Examine your daily routine today and find out where your time is spent. When you pray, is it all about you and your family? We must make sure that we are doing what is needful and not according to what we esteem as important.

Day 20

Self-Examination

"But if we would examine ourselves, we would not be judged by God in this way." I Corinthians 11:30 NLT

In order for us to get to that place in worship, we must first examine ourselves and return back to him. When we find ourselves distant from God, we must take a good look at us and find out where we went wrong. Worship is an ongoing experience with God but can be interrupted by our flesh and desires. Just like the prodigal son, he had to come to himself and realize he had sinned against his father. He had to return and repent.

When we repent, we recognize that we have done wrong and we need to turn from it. In our worship, we don't want anything to separate us and we know sin keeps us separated from God. We must die daily and checking ourselves to make sure we're in right standing with God is what we do often. Let us examine ourselves so that we don't miss what God desires to give.

Today's application: Take the time to look back over the past twenty days. Have you improved in any area? What do you need to work on? What has changed? If you feel the need to ask for forgiveness, this is the perfect time to do so. God is always available for us and he waits to hear from us daily. Dying is process and no one arrives overnight. When you take the time to do the work, the results are guaranteed. As you proceed, continue to apply that which you have learned and keep pressing toward the mark.

Day 21

Humble Yourselves

"Humble yourselves therefore under the mighty hand of God, that he may exalt you in due time." I Peter 5:6 KJV

When people say that they are humble, they associate that with them being in the background or not having a whole lot of things. They shy away from the spotlight and think less of themselves. That is not what it means to be humble. It does not require us to degrade ourselves, but it gives an opportunity for others to take notice of the gifts and talents we have. Everyone can not be in the background and that doesn't make us the humblest person because we don't stand out front. Being humble is about always being the student even if you are the teacher.

It is having an attitude to work with anyone regardless of what they may bring to the table, in order to give others the opportunity to showcase what they can do. It is about being confident in whom we are and not becoming puffed up to make others look bad. We have to be able to take direction as well as lead. Christ was considered humble because he came down from glory and put on flesh so that he could be the example to follow. He was the king but became the servant. That is what we should consider humble.

When we die to self, we put on the servants attire and serve everyone the same. No matter the title, we have a purpose and plan to fulfill. Remaining humble even when we are right shows that we see the bigger picture. We apologize even when we have done nothing wrong. It is always about others regardless the situation. God exalts those who are humble in due time. If we die to self, elevation is automatic in the lives of those who carry their cross.

Today's application: Don't continue to sit at the back because you are trying to look humble. Be who you are and allow God to place you where you belong. Keep your hands clean from mischief and go throughout your day knowing that in due season, the Lord will raise you up. Don't be quick to be seen but be someone people remember. Not by your excessive words, but by your ability to adapt to any situation.

Day 22

You Are a Friend

Greater love hath no man than this, that a man would lay down his life for his friends. (John 15:13)

Friends, how many of us have them? Friends, the ones we can depend on. This is a popular song that gets us to thinking about the company we keep. Everyone we come in contact with is not a friend and we must show ourselves friendly in order to know what that even looks like. Friendships are developed through relationship. We must spend time with each other in order to truly know a person. Friends share and confide in each other and they are also honest with one another. Friends tell the truth even if it means hurting their feelings in order to save their life. We know that Jesus called his disciples his friends because whatever God revealed to him, Jesus revealed to them. He walked with them and shared everything. He withheld nothing. They were all on the same team. He gained their trust and he helped them get to where they needed to be. He gave of himself freely and in return they gave of themselves when Jesus returned to the Father.

How do we treat our friends? Do we simply tolerate them until we find someone better? Is it all about us? Do we withhold things from them? When we say that Jesus is our friend, how are we treating him? We can't worship or become intimate with someone you're not friends with. We tolerate or put up with them because it's still all about you. If Jesus is our friend, why is it so hard for us to die? Jesus gave up his life for his friends so they would be saved. What have we done for our friends lately?

Today's application: If we were to interview your friends, what would they reveal about you? Would they speak highly of you or would they have some things to share that you would not want anyone to hear? Let us make sure we are showing the spirit of Christ at all times so that we can be counted as one of his friends.

Day 23

God's Helpmeet

"And the Lord God said, it is not good that the man should be alone; I will make him a help meet for him." Genesis 2:18 KJV

When we think about a helpmeet, we automatically think about a wife. I will make him a Helpmeet is one of the most defining sentences of our time. Many people know that God was referring to woman when he spoke these words. He saw that Adam needed help. God created woman to help or assist her husband in any way that she could. She was to meet the need that may have been asked of her. She was to help carry out the plans that were already laid before them. As a worshiper, you are committing to being God's Help meet.

If Christ is the husbandman, we are the bride. He needs our help in getting the will of God into the earth. This means that we have the same mindset and the same desire as he does. Worship requires a submission to the purpose and plan that has already been ordained by God. We freely give of ourselves and become one. We take pleasure in standing with God to make sure he succeeds in his mission. We're not concerned with your own agenda because we understand the importance of not our will, but your will be done. God needs us to help get the word to those who are lost. If we're not willing to help, then we won't meet or complete the requirements for worship.

Today's application: See yourself as God's help meet. What has he asked of you that you may not have agreed to? You must be willing to give of yourself in order for the work to be completed. If you are not sure, ask him what your part is. It will take you working with him for it to be accomplished.

Day 24

Heart of Compassion

"Finally, be ye all of one mind, having compassion one of another, love as brethren, be pitiful, be courteous." I Peter 3:8 KJV

We often are shown in the scriptures where Jesus was moved with compassion for the great multitudes. His heart was moved by what he saw and felt concerning the people. Many times they are found wondering and scattered abroad. Because of his devotion to God, he healed and taught the people to make sure they knew about the love of God. He made it his mission to help anyone who was in need.

Having compassion for people is a mindset to help. No one person can help everyone and that is why Jesus had disciples. It is a selfless act of kindness to see your brother or sister in a better state of mind. Showing compassion means we care about their needs and have a desire to help. You will find a way to give so that others can live. You will give people what they need. Using the gifts and talents God has given us, we should want to rescue as many people we can from hell. That is what Jesus came to do. He came to heal us and restore us back to our rightful place. If we are more concerned about us and not compassionate about others, we have lost the meaning of the cross.

Today's application: Compassion doesn't mean to be everything to everyone but to be moved to do something. Don't turn the other cheek but seek God on how you can be of some service to someone today. Buying someone some lunch or taking the time to listen is all it takes. We all have something we can give. Just be willing to do so when the Father touches your heart to do it.

Day 25

Follow the Leader

"The Lord says, I will guide you along the best pathway for your life. I will advise you and watch over you." Psalm 32:8 NLT

Do you remember the game follow the leader? How good were you at this game? Was it a challenge because you always wanted to lead or were you ok with following? In order to worship, we must first know how to follow. We must learn to come behind Christ and be comfortable in him leading us. I know we have been taught to be independent and take care of ourselves but what does God require and want from us? He wants to lead us on the best path that was designed specifically for us.

We must be willing to pursue or follow behind his leadership. If we're always coming up with a separate plan or a plan B, we are not fully trusting God or following after his wisdom. We must drop our independent ways and be willing to be led or guided by God. True disciples understand the importance of following. They put aside their own agenda and deny themselves. We can't follow if we're always in the lead.

Today's application: Allow the Holy Spirit to you in all that you do throughout the day. Listen carefully for his voice in your surroundings. God is constantly speaking to us in ways that we will understand. You must be willing to let go and let God.

Day 26

Worship through Praise

"And I, if I be lifted up from the earth, will draw all men unto me." John 12:32 KJV

Praise can be considered the highest form of a compliment. When we praise someone, we acknowledge that they have done a superb job. We are usually impressed and satisfied with the work they have provided. We recommend them to our family and friends and we stand by their work. If we are on our job and our boss begins to speak highly of our performance, it is because they approve of the way that we carry ourselves and the work we have completed. Through praise, you highlight the strengths and the ability of another.

Worshiping God with praise is verbally speaking about him in a way that shows that we approve of him and all that he has done for us. We speak highly of him to others and we recommend him to them. We stand by him and his ability to perform. Our praise should never be withheld or silenced because of something he did not do for us when we wanted him to. We have enough evidence about him to praise him through eternity. The more we praise him or speak highly of him, the more people are drawn to our God. We cannot praise someone we do not believe in and we can't worship someone we don't approve of.

Today's application: Let today be a day where you praise God or share your testimony. People need to hear you speak highly of the God you serve. Don't be afraid of their faces. You don't know what your words will do for someone until you open your mouth. Give others an opportunity to hear him in a way that they would want to know him for themselves.

Day 27

Communicate Through Prayer

"Devote yourself to prayer with an alert mind and a thankful heart." Colossians 4:2 KJV

One day I conducted a survey where I asked people what they considered to be the top five things you must have in order to have a successful relationship. The number one response was communication. This is the area where many fall short because we don't know how to effectively say what's on our minds. How will we know what the other person is thinking or feeling if we don't communicate? Prayer is what we do to stay connected to God and we are asked to do it without ceasing. How will we know which way to go if we don't talk with God? If we stop communicating with him, we will find ourselves leaning unto our own understanding. Prayer is where we receive our wise counsel.

When we decide not to consult God, we find ourselves out of synch with each other and we give room for the enemy and the flesh to take over. God expects us to seek him in everything and to express our concerns with him first. We don't consult with outside sources before we consult with your mate so why would we consult others before we talk with God? Open lines of communication will keep us in perfect peace and will eliminate unwanted frustration if we learn to be honest and open with God. Worship keeps you before God. If we don't talk with him, we lose sight of where you are going.

Today's application: Don't stop communicating. It does not matter what goes on throughout this day. Continue to talk with the one you are serving because he will tell you what you need to do. He is always ready for a conversation with you. If you leave him out, how will you know what to do or what's on his heart. Prayer is dialogue, not just a monologue.

Day 28

Pleasing God Matters

"By faith, Enoch was translated that he should not see death; and was not found, because God had translated him: for before his translation he had this testimony, that he pleased God." Hebrews 11:5 KJV

Worship is a one on one relationship that focuses on God. It is meeting God's needs and doing what pleases him. There are a lot of things we think will please him because it makes us happy. The only way we will know is if we spend time in his presence.

God is a jealous God and we should put no other God before him. In Hebrews 11:5 it says Enoch pleased God. Everything he did lined up with God. He didn't worry about what was popular, who wasn't doing it or who approved or disapproved. His heart was toward God. His testimony spoke of his love and devotion for God. He didn't allow people or anything to get him to turn away from him and that pleased God. He agreed with God. He was happy and content with God. He wasn't looking for something better but longing to know him more.

How can we worship someone when we are not concerned about their heart or what they need? We are so quick to ask God to please us but when was the last time we really made it all about him? Does your worship please God? Enoch pleased God in such a way that God came and took him. He made God feel so important, he didn't even allow death to take him. Think about that. If we set out to please God with everything in us, we will never see death.

Today's application: Make up in your mind to please God at all cost. We must be ready at all times to do or say whatever will bring joy to our Father's heart. Don't be afraid to please him because in return, you will receive the heart and the hand of God in your life.

Day 29

Faith is Worship

"But without faith it is impossible to please him."
Hebrews 11:6 KJV

According to Hebrews 11:1, it says that now faith is the substance of things hoped for, the evidence of things not seen. We also understand that by faith the worlds were formed by God's word. Nothing we set out to do can be accomplished without faith. Faith is the foundation on which God stands on. Wherever faith is, fear isn't. God expects his children to lean and depend on him for everything. We will not have a lot of details when it comes to walking by faith but it will get us to our destination every time.

If we're going to walk with God, we must do it by faith and not fear. Fear is attached to our flesh which will limit our obedience and our worship. Fear won't allow us to make bold steps towards God's plan for our lives. Faith is the currency of heaven and is only recognized by God. We must believe that he is God and we trust him with all of our heart. There will be times where our faith is tested. It is not to cripple us but to create an atmosphere of advancement into the supernatural. The more you hear and obey God, the more our faith will increase.

We know that faith cometh by hearing and hearing by the word of God. This is why the relationship and prayer is vital to a faith walk. We will not know what to do if we don't take the time to hear God through his word. Faith allows us to go places we would never be able to go with fear. Standing strong in our faith like Abraham will deliver the promises of God in our lives. If we can develop a life of faith, we will tap into kingdom living.

Today's application: Take a leap of faith today towards the goals you have heard God speak of concerning your life. How will you know if it will work if you won't have the faith to do the impossible? God is with you and anything he ask of you, he has the ability to back it up. Put fear out of your mind and start taking the steps toward your freedom in Christ.

Day 30

Persevere and Endure

"Stay with God! Take heart. Don't quit. I'll say it again: Stay with God. Psalm 27:14 MSG

When we're walking with God, many things will come our way to stop us or slow down the process. Many people will question us because it must not be God if we're suffering like this. We're facing opposition on every side and it doesn't look as if it's ever going to end. In order for us to persevere, our faith and trust must be in God. We will not be able to handle it alone. Our flesh can't handle the pressure.

When we commit to worship in the spirit, we're being driven by the resurrection power of God and you are strengthened and graced to endure. Dying to self is the only way we will make it through to the other side. Your ability to continue even though we're feeling the opposition shows your commitment to worship God.

Daily, the enemy comes to steal, kill and destroy. He doesn't care how he does it but his goal is to create an atmosphere that will convince us that it is not worth it. We must remember that all things are working for your good and they are working together. God will take a bad situation and make it work in our favor. If we faint not, we will receive all that he has promised us. He will not fail us. If we have the faith to believe that all things are possible, our ability to endure will sky rocket us beyond our wildest dreams.

Today's application: No matter what, don't stop pressing. The press is to produce a level of power in your life to help deliver others. God is with you and you have all that you need to keep going. Don't focus on your situation but focus on the one who is able to turn it around at any moment.

Day 31

Willing to Sacrifice

"Then Peter began to say unto him, Lo, we have left all, and have followed thee." Mark 10:28 KJV

Sacrifice is about giving up what we desire, want or have in our possession to follow after God. When the disciples made the decision to drop everything and follow Jesus, they didn't understand the extent of the sacrifice but they knew it was necessary. We can't be too attached to this world and worship God. We must be willing to let go or give up anything or anyone in order to fulfill God's plan and purpose in the Earth. Sacrifice is necessary for our growth and it brings us closer to God.

He won't ask us to give up anything that he doesn't intend on giving back but it will be what he wants to give us. God is not mocked. Whatever we sow or sacrifice, we shall reap. So what are we willing to give up? Sometimes God will ask us to give up something to show us where our heart is. If God is requiring it, it must be something we hold dear to our heart that will hinder the flow of his spirit. If we remain in this state of mind, we are not fully convinced that the sacrifice is necessary for worship.

God is not just taking things away from us because he wants us to go without but he wants us to depend less on ourselves and those that are around us. If we are going to walk with God, we can't have crutches on standby. He needs us to be able to walk away from anything at any given moment because the purpose is bigger than the sacrifice. We must be willing to release it and be confident to know if we let it go, what he has is far greater than anything we could have done for ourselves.

Today's application: What are you willing to sacrifice? What are you willing to live without? We cannot allow anything to separate us from his love or his will. God loves a cheerful giver. Sacrifice is a desire to receive more from God in order to bring healing to those in need.

Day 32

Have a Grateful Attitude

"What shall I render unto the Lord for all of his benefits toward me?" Psalm 116:12 KJV

Being grateful is worship. It means that we appreciate God for what he has done and we don't take him for granted. God has done so much for us that if we were honest, we would not have time to be ungrateful. If we think back to last night, he kept us all night long. He protected us. He has given us brand new mercies. He has forgiven our sins and sent his Son to die in our place.

Instead of thanking him or being grateful that he didn't allow that relationship to work or job to come through because he saw something we didn't or wouldn't see, we complain and blame him because of our misery. We don't thank him for blocking the worst mistake of our lives. We are quick to forget that he has fed us, gave us garments to wear, healed us over and over again, provided for us, protected us and made a way out of no way. We are just concerned with now and what we want.

Let me ask you something. If we're in a committed relationship and the other person never acknowledges what we've done or appreciate us but always wanting more, how would we feel? Be honest. Our feelings would be hurt. They never have anything nice to say about us to others especially their family. Anything that we do is never good enough. They are always talking about what we haven't done and hardly mention the good things.

When we spend time complaining about what isn't right, we have stepped out of worship and back into self. God can't accept or acknowledge that kind of worship because it goes against what he stands for. We must remember what he's done and remain grateful. We understand that God is able to take care of our present just like he did your past. Our gratitude draws us closer to him and gets him to move on our behalf.

Today's application: Show God how much you appreciate him by learning to be content. Look at where you are and where you have come from. See him in everything and just begin to praise him. Take care of the things you already have. Be a good steward with your finances, home, car and the clothes you presently have. Take care of your body in a way that will please him. This is how we show him how grateful we are for all that he has done.

Day 33

Worship through Thanksgiving

"And when ye will offer a sacrifice of Thanksgiving unto the Lord, offer it at your own will." Leviticus 22:29 KJV

As previously stated, prayer is an essential part of worship. Prayer is how we communicate with God. It is during this time we get to know him, his ways and also to express our concerns and confessions. Thanksgiving is giving thanks unto God through our intimate time with him. When we are in his presence, he wants to hear us give him thanks. Just like being grateful, we show our appreciation to God and this is a sign that we understand that we did none of this on our own.

We understand that in him we live, move and have our being. When we were young, we were taught to say thank you when someone gives us something. If we failed to say it, we were checked real quick and reminded that I didn't have to do it but I did. This is how we should act with God. We must be ready to express to him how much we love him for because continues to do for us even when we don't do for him.

How often do we say thank you or tell him how much we appreciate him for all of his goodness? Do you always have list for God or are we spending majority of our time giving thanks? How often do we speak about him that is a direct reflection of his character or ability? Do we give thanks in all things? Thanksgiving is something we live, not a once a year gathering around food. Everyday should be a day of thanks. Don't get so caught up in what we have going on that you forget who helped us get to that place.

Today's application: In all things give thanks. Make today all about his goodness and his mercy he has shown us this day. Tell him thank you throughout the day. Whenever anything crosses your mind, just simply say Lord I thank you.

Day 34

Suffering is Worship

"Yea, and all that will live godly in Christ Jesus shall suffer persecution." II Timothy 3:12 KJV

When we think of worship, suffering isn't something that we would normally associate with it but suffering is a requirement for worship. When we worship, we are devoted and committed to God. It's not about us anymore and if we're going to be in this relationship for the long haul, we will have to suffer.

When we are standing at the altar and the preacher reads the vows, for better or for worse, suffering is part of it. No relationship will ever go without testing or trials. We will have troubles simply because we have chosen to follow Christ and if he suffered, who are we to think we can skip that part and go straight to the promises of God.

So what does that mean? If we make the decision to follow Christ or worship, the enemy is going to try to do everything he can to get us to deny him. Remember Job? He was a righteous man who was faced with every affliction possible because the enemy wanted him to curse God and die. Job was living right but because he stood for what was right, he was a target.

If we're going to reign with Christ, we will suffer with him as well. Even in that, we still have the victory. Dying to self is a daily sacrifice. Worship is a lifestyle and persecution will come but endure as a good soldier. God believes in us. That's why we were chosen! Don't focus so much on the suffering. It's temporary! Be of good cheer because Jesus has already overcome the world.

Today's application: Whatever you're going, make sure it's for the sake of the gospel and not because you are being a busy body in others affairs. Count it all joy when these things come up against you. Give God some praise for even being counted among the righteous. This is not the time to have a pity party but praise parties knowing you are headed in the right direction.

Day 35

Remaining Faithful through Worship

"He staggered not at the promise of God through unbelief; but was strong in faith, giving glory to God." Romans 4:20 KJV

Remaining faithful in a world full of infidelity has become a lost art. No one wants to stick around when the going gets tough. We are quick to back away from anything that requires work. We expect things to go the way we want and if it doesn't, we run for the hills and we don't look back. Loyalty is just a word to many and if it doesn't satisfy our wants when we want them, we will leave and go somewhere that will give us what we want in the time frame we have allotted. We have become a world that is accustomed to the microwave that we don't have a desire to wait for anything.

Worship is recognized when we are being faithful to God and fully convinced of his ability to produce. We are able to stand with him when there is no proof and not turning our back on him or doubting his plan. We believe in him and remain by his side no matter what.

Being faithful to God through worship is being faithful to the relationship. We continuously support his ideas, plans and purpose. We don't allow the lack of understanding to keep us from following through with what we have committed to. Supporting him and standing with him is huge in the relationship and our inability to stand with him will make others apprehensive about worshiping God. How loyal and faithful we are will help others receive from God and see him for who he really is.

Today's application: Don't allow anything to separate you from the love of God. He has so much more in store for you that you have to stay with him in order to get it. Block out anything that is not truth and think on things that are of a good report. Remember, trouble don't last always.

Day 36

Showing Godly Behavior

"Wherefore, my beloved brethren, let every man be swift to hear, slow to speak, slow to wrath." James 1:19 KJV

Even though we are in the world, we should not be of the world. The world shows us how to treat our neighbors by manipulating them and doing whatever it takes to get to the top even if it means behaving in a way that isn't always the nicest. It's all about self-gratification and no matter how much it affects others, people will only look out for themselves.

Worshiping God requires us to conduct ourselves in a manner that pleases God at all times. We should not want to bring shame to his name regardless of how others treat us. If we respect God, you're mindful of what you say and do. We should be careful to respond in a way that will not taint our testimony. Our actions should line up with our words. We must pray for those who spitefully use us and also love our enemies. We are different from the world and how we treat them should be different.

Remember, how we conduct ourselves in the presence of others should be a reflection of the God we serve. We may be the only Jesus they see. Make sure we are portraying him in a way that will draw others to him and not away from him.

Today's application: Make sure you are behaving in a way that if Jesus was standing next to you, he would be pleased. There is never a time that we can justify our actions because of the way we were treated. Be careful not to give yourself or your God a bad name. You want people to be able to come to you because of the light that is within. How you behave will either compel them or repel them.

Day 37

Worship with Love

"Love never gives up, never loses faith, is always hopeful, and endures through every circumstance." I Corinthians 13:7 NLT

Love is a four letter word that is getting bad press because we truly don't know what it is. Love is patient and kind and never demands its own way. It gives more than it takes and never keeps a record of wrong doing. It is always ready to lend a helping hand and it doesn't mind putting others before itself. It isn't puffed up and doesn't think more highly of itself than it ought. It sacrifices for the sake of others and is willing to lay down its life at all cost. We have confused love with lust because we constantly are operating from a place of me and not from a place of He.

When we worship God, we are constantly thinking about him. Our love for him will keep us with him through every situation. We don't give up neither do we lose our faith during the process.

When we worship, we love someone else with our all. For God so loved the world that he gave us his son. He gave us ALL of him. He didn't give up on us because of our ways. He remained hopeful and faithful. That's love and adoration. If we're going to worship God, we can't throw in the towel because things get hard. Love will keep us right by his side. We show a person how much we love them through our actions. It's not always about our presence but our prayers are never absent. Worship turns us toward God and deepens our love for him especially through the hard times. How deep is our love?

Today's application: Allow his love to take you beyond the limits. Let love rule your heart and give of yourself in ways you have never done before. Show your spouse, parent, co-worker or friends how much you love them today by doing something random you know they will appreciate. Don't put love in a box. Be free to be open to others. Let love have its perfect work for love covers a multitude of sin.

Day 38

Surrender to Worship

"Therefore, since we are surrounded by such a huge crowd of witnesses to the life of faith, let us strip off every weight that slows us down, especially the sin that so easily trips us up. And let us run with endurance the race God has set before us." Hebrews 12:1 NLT

One of the hardest things to do is to surrender or lay down something. We hold on to so much that we can sometimes forget that we are still carrying around some weights. It has become our normal place to be burdened that we don't know how it feels not to carry a load. It is not our intention but it does happen from time to time. To fully worship God, we must become weightless.

Surrender means to agree to stop fighting, hiding or resisting because we, will not win or succeed. It also means to give the control to someone else. We have to be willing to get out of the driver's seat and hand the keys over to God. We have been in this place for so long, it is a struggle that we face each and every day. Letting go of control is showing God that we trust him and his plan for our life. This is where we are waving the little white flag and signaling our opponent that they win because they are too much for them to handle anymore.

God will never force his ways on us. He desires that we surrender under our own free will so that we don't feel as though we were pressured to do something we were not ready to do. Even though he shows us a better way, it is still up to us to relinquish the rights we have to ourselves. We must be willing to surrender or lay down anything that will hinder our worship to God. Worship is about bowing and agreeing with God. Extra weight will keep us from doing that. Let's examine ourselves so that we are not carrying around anything that is not necessary or beneficial on your journey.

Today's application: What extra baggage are you carrying around that you have not surrendered to God? Have you surrendered yourself for his using? In order to die, you must present yourself as the sacrifice because you believe that it is necessary. Don't continue to hold out because you are afraid of what might happen. Give God the chance to show you what he has for you. You will not be disappointed.

Day 39

Submission Is Key

"Do not be stubborn, as they were, but submit yourselves to the Lord. Come to his Temple, which he has set apart as holy forever. Worship the Lord your God so that his fierce anger will turn away from you."
II Chronicles 30:8 NLT

Submission is that ugly word that man has used against women in order to get what they want. Whenever a woman hears the world submission, she immediately goes into defense mode of how she doesn't need someone bossing her around because she can think and do for herself. Men think that submission is not a part of their job description and is sometimes looked as beneath them as well. We should get rid of those man made definitions because submitting to God is far from someone just bossing you around or having complete rule and reign over you.

Submission in worship means to come under God's wing and allow him to lead us in all things. We are now under his umbrella so that he can provide for us and be all that we need him to be. A person still operating in the flesh will not be able to do this because they will still feel the need to control and dictate. There is an order to Gods calling and we must be willing to relinquish our rights over to him. If we can't fully commit to God, we will always hold back from the people we are meant to serve. Our relationships will always be rocky.

A worshiper is devoted to the things of God. He understands that in all his ways he acknowledges God and he directs his path. That is why he ask us to seek ye first the kingdom of God. God is always trying to add unto us and submission allows things to be added. We don't want to lose out because we believe that we have a better way of doing things. There is a death in submission that will take us to our next level. Don't delay the request being made. It will benefit us in the long run.

Today's application: Begin to see yourself under the wing of God. Know that he has great things in store for those who are willing to join him in his purpose. Submission doesn't make you weak but it shows you how strong you are in the Lord.

Day 40

Obedience is Worship

"But Samuel replied, what is more pleasing to the Lord: Your burnt offerings and sacrifices or your obedience to his voice? Listen! Obedience is better than sacrifice, and submission is better than offering the fat of rams." I Samuel 15:22 NLT

Obedience is always better than sacrifice. Even though worship requires sacrifice, one must obey the word when it is spoken. The bible says not to be a hearer only but a doer as well. When God ask anything of us, it is through our obedience that we receive the abundance of our blessings. Obedience brings deliverance. Obedience will make the difference between reward and wrath. Obedience must always accompany our worship lifestyle so that the plans of God can be fulfilled.

Obedience separates the holy from the unholy. Obedience is about denying anyone including ourselves and following after the things that God has declared. We must be bold and unapologetic and stand firm on that which we know he has said. Obedience strengthens our faith and brings hope to those who have become hopeless. God honors those who honor his word.

It was through the disobedience of one that the world knew of sin and it was the obedience of one who brought salvation unto the world. Our obedience is the lifeline for someone else. We have to be able to think about others if we want to live a life of obedience to God. There is life attached to our obedience and we can bring so much life to those around us by simply telling God yes. Don't under estimate the power that our yes possesses.

Someone is waiting on our obedience to God. We all have a responsibility to uphold and the sooner we die to ourselves, the sooner we will see a mighty move of God in the land. Being able to deny ourselves and take up our cross shows Christ we are ready for what he has in store for us.

Today's application: Obey God even when it doesn't make sense. You are about to embark on a new journey and obedience must be a part of your daily confession. Learn to listen and respond quickly. God is looking for those who have a yes in their heart and will yield everything suddenly. Obedience allows you to yield.

Conclusion

Although today marks the end of the 40 days of worship, it is the beginning of your next level. When we walked through these 40 days, it was something we may have never experienced. Now that we have a better understanding of what true worship is, we can begin to live a life that will please god and benefit others.

This came at a time where I knew God wanted to increase my wisdom and knowledge of who he is but some things were still in the way. I had not died all the way. It wasn't that I was doing something really wrong or intentionally sinning, but there would come a time where my death was going to have to take place and the beginning of this year was the perfect time to do it.

He gave me what to write down and work on every day and now it has become a part of me. I know this is may be just a book but this is what we should strive to do every day of our lives. God is so gracious and merciful unto us that he expects us to do the same with our fellow brothers and sisters. We should not take it likely the opportunities he has afforded us and the keys he has left for us to unlock the mysteries. I am forever thankful and grateful for all that he has done for me.

As you continue on your journey, don't forget to enjoy it. Death is a part of life and one day we all will go in the physical. Dying to the flesh can be painful but in due time, you will understand why it needed to happen. We can become stuck if we focus more on the death than the life that will be resurrected through our unselfishness. God is with us every step of the way and we never have to worry about doing this walk on our own. I am excited about your future with him and if you allow him the chance to show you his plan, you will never regret it. Let go of this world so that you can live the life you were created to live from the beginning. I believe in you and we need each other. Keep pressing toward the mark and you will soon receive the prize of the high calling in Christ Jesus. In order to live, there must be a death.

Extra Nuggets

*Being able to have self-control comes from being intentional about worship and staying in the spirit. A person cannot blame their immaturity on the lack of another person showing them the attention they desire. One must be able to handle themselves no matter what someone else does or doesn't. Using their faults as a crutch to continue with wreck less behavior doesn't say much about them but it does reflect your level to handle situations under pressure. A person must look themselves directly in the eye and take full responsibility for their actions.

*No one should have that much control or power over you. If a person can get that much out of you, how much more would you give if you allowed God full control? He wants to take all of that and make it work for your good. Stay in the spirit. When those emotions come, speak to them and put them back in check. Don't allow them to take over and drive. You will end up somewhere you didn't intend to go. Once you get there, it may be hard to get back.

*Don't allow someone else guilt to hinder you from progressing. Everybody that wants to be heard doesn't want to be helped. A NO will help you decide who you are dealing with.

*If you are feeling the pain from an emotional drive by, know that the bullet wasn't for you. They were trying to kill their past but you got caught in the crossfire. Instead of confronting their past, it resurfaced when they least expected it and they panicked. You were there and when they fired at their past, they hit you. The damage that was done before you had nothing to do with you.

*Many times people refuse to face their past, and end up killing their future. Know that you did nothing wrong. The emotional bullet may have hit major nerves and arteries, but you are expected to live. Recovery will be a process but the healing will take place. The surgeon has entered the operating room and he will remove every bullet you took. Don't worry. The evidence of a scar will be minimal but the wound will be healed. Even though the enemy tried his best to take you out, the love you have shielded you. So be encouraged for you will live to love again.

*If your mind doesn't want to surrender, your body will not be offered up.

*Purposed Love does not make you feel paranoid. God is intentional and straight forward with his love for you. Believe it!

*God will not speed up the process to your promise land to pacify your insecurities. Matter of fact, he will slow it down so you can face them, be delivered from them and effectively cross over.

*Rushing the process doesn't make it official. Once the word is spoken by God, it's already done.

*Stop giving your insecurities the microphone! They no longer speak for you.

*Sometimes God will allow people to show up in your life just to reveal to you an area that still needed to be worked on. One day you may look around and they are no longer there. Don't be mad at them. It was their assignment from God. They helped you get closer to your destiny. Even Judas got Jesus closer to his purpose. Don't hold them accountable for the heart ache but thank God for the growth.

*Don't bring worldly thinking into a God ordained relationship. You are no longer there and should not respond according to that place. You may not think you're ready but if God brings you to it, his grace will see you through it and the Holy Ghost will teach you all that you need to know in order to succeed.

*Don't let your past paralyze your purpose!

*At some point, you have to stop saying why you and start believing it is you. If God intended for you to have it, be it or achieve it, he has the right one in mind! Just say thank you and walk in it!

*Don't miss what God is doing because you are not use to it. Receive what you have prayed for in secret. God is rewarding you openly. Your past could not comprehend who you were. Your future is well aware that's why he is making himself known.

*Celebrate the person in front of you when God blesses them. Don't allow envy or jealousy to make you get out of line. Why? Because if you're that close to see them getting blessed, it means you're next!

*If you are constantly looking for a round of applause from man, you will miss your standing ovation from God.

*If God is showing you your purpose in the spirit, don't go back to the natural and compromise! Don't allow what you see or going through to stop what God has already shown you!! It's not according to what you see, it's according to what he said!!! It's moving time.

*You can't worship God thinking about you.

*Pleasing God will get you a well done.

*If you're the smartest person in the room, start teaching.

*Forgiveness is necessary and a prerequisite for greater works.

*If you take care of God's house, he will take care of yours.

Made in the USA
San Bernardino, CA
15 January 2017